The Mental Illness Handbook

A Guide for Professionals

B. N. Christopher

Law of Statement:

"My concern was that "mental illness" is defined metaphysically (subjectively, psychosocially) rather than scientifically (objectively, physically), which means any research involving "mental illness" hinges, in part, on non-scientific value judgements. The people writing the DSM say things like that psychiatric diagnoses are "bullshit", many articles favorable to industry gains are ghostwritten, and there appears to be a near-unanimous agreement that current structures are causing a lot of preventable harms. Most funding for this research comes from vested interest parties, not people who fundamentally care whether or not "mental illness" is defined in a particular way or responded to in a particular manner. Psychosocial rubrics are like the psychiatric equivalent of Christians saying "well, in the Bible…" when addressing objective issues like the fossil record or epigenetic heritance. It is objectively true that certain statements are contained within the Bible. Their veracity and relevance are what is under debate in this sort of context, to speak analogously. "Mental illness" remains a non-scientific entity, which is currently incapable of being the subject of scientific research. We would need a scientific definition of "mental illness" (or specific respective diagnoses) before 'hard research' could be performed. Rubrics with no objective value in establishing the presence of a causal physical entity are not talking about "mental illness" in an 'actually real' way. I am not saying that leaves us nowhere. Clearly, there is something handy to this whole 'psychology' thing. I think it would be even more effectual if it stopped trying to create marketing hype about being scientific. The public is willing to shell out for things claiming to be scientific, I do realize. But

undermining the potency of the paradigm through misrepresentation and bastardization is not a sustainable practice if we do indeed hope to preserve psychology rather than some sort of mass media interpretation of human existence. I am heavily in favor of using the right tools for the right jobs. Sometimes science is the right tool, sometimes it is not. Sometimes psychology is the right tool, sometimes it is not. I totally agree that research ought to be about adding to human knowledge and efficacy. But, most research is about economic returns, and the people performing, documenting, or publishing it may not think it's accurate or 'real' at all. Since "knowledge" expands in all directions, even ideas which are objectively wrong or subjectively wrong are an increase in human knowledge, so that is not so much a limitation on the increase as it is on the motivations and outcomes. There is, of course, no shortage of researchers genuinely interested in pure inquiry, or even applied inquiry outside of financial gain. They face the obstacle of an unsupportive cultural and economic environment, however, and instead, the peer-reviewed medical journals are chock full of chucklehead studies which are basically just the marketing department of vested interest parties. The primary impetus behind codified human knowledge right now is in conflict with an honest and ethically sound search for truth. (Or, in the case of science, search for better-fitting theories.)"

~Anonymous

The Mental Illness Handbook

Author's Note:

The information presented in this handbook has been provided for the intention to acknowledge those who either have had, or still have, an objectively-based mental disorder. In any case, this handbook is not designed to be read by someone interpreted as being mentally ill. That being said, this publication should be utilized by a trusted source, not by someone with the likelihood of psychologically harming these types of individuals. This necessitates the requirement for the reader to be well-versed in the information provided; in the event that they do intend to provide assistance for any mentally-disordered individual.

On another note, the author would like to thank an undergraduate teaching assistant in late 2015, at Bunker Hill Community College (Boston, Massachusetts) for being notably involved in the realization that people with borderline personality disorder functioned in respects to that of a closed-world assumption. In addition to this, it should be noted that further research took place separately between faculties in that school (with the exception of the department(s) in this/these field(s) of study) and the author. Confirmations, including direct discussions with the author, were solely done with one other person.

Table of Contents:

Section 6: Additional Concepts

Section 1: Misplacement Chart

1.1 INTRODUCTION

The purpose of this handbook is to set forward an alternative definition to the concept of mental illness, and to establish a guide for assistance when dealing with someone who is mentally ill. To do this, an assumed definition is provided for the intention to guide professionals in a way that would allow for a better establishment in understanding and applying useful concepts that can, in turn, benefit their clients.

For the intention of this handbook, a cause, description, and treatment for a listing of disorders are explicitly given. However, this listing agrees on the terms that a mental disorder is to be defined by *a boundary that is indicative of an impairment in at least one of thirteen categories on the misplacement chart*. This definition intends to serve as a better ground for the information provided in this handbook, such that, it would fit in conjunction with the use to clarify and establish mental illness in an objectively real way (Frances, 2013a, p. 221-2).

1.2 RECOGNIZED LABEL IN DISORDER

But before we discuss more in regards to the misplacement chart, let's take a step back and mention what led to the creation of the chart itself. To clarify, this idea came about with an observation of various occurrences in the given population, in which a fraction of individuals were founded to have underwent a psychologically-caused impairment, resulting in an alteration in their own behavior. This observation is what sparked a proposed categorization in order to help classify that given demographic.

However, one roadblock came about when utilizing how to refer to a particular mental disorder. Since the nature of the disorders prohibited the ability to use its own cause as a label of reference, previously held labels that closely allied to the experience of the disorders were used instead. Therefore, any label that's mentioned in this handbook serves for the sole purpose of giving recognition to what a client is exclusively experiencing. It does not intend to serve in conjunction with any of the descriptions provided in the Diagnostic and Statistical Manual of Mental Disorders (4th ed., text rev.; DSM–IV–TR; American Psychiatric

Association, 2000), regardless of any similarities that it may exhibit. As a result of this, a listing of disorders were identified through the use of the definition provided. This listing, in comparison to the resulting labels taken from the DSM-IV-TR, is shown below:

Avoidant Personality Disorder	Repressed Guilt
Unrecognized Mental Disorder	Suppressed Guilt
Antisocial Personality Disorder	Repressed Remorse
Histrionic Personality Disorder	Suppressed Remorse
Depersonalization Disorder	Repressed Paranoia
Dissociative Identity Disorder	Suppressed Paranoia
Borderline Personality Disorder	Repressed Special
Unrecognized Mental Disorder	Suppressed Special
Schizoid Personality Disorder	Repressed Apathy
Schizotypal Personality Disorder	Suppressed Apathy
Dependent Personality Disorder	Repressed Worry
Obsessive-Compulsive Personality Disorder	Suppressed Worry
Unrecognized Mental Disorder	Repressed Envy
Unrecognized Mental Disorder	Suppressed Envy
Unrecognized Mental Disorder	Repressed Jealousy
Unrecognized Mental Disorder	Suppressed Jealousy

Unrecognized Mental Disorder	Repressed Anger
Unrecognized Mental Disorder	Suppressed Anger
Intermittent Explosive Disorder	Repressed Fear
Paranoid Personality Disorder	Suppressed Fear
Dissociative Amnesia	Repressed Arousal
Dissociative Fugue	Suppressed Arousal
Bipolar Type I Disorder	Repressed Boredom
Bipolar Type II Disorder	Suppressed Boredom
PTSD (Fight or Flight)	Invalidated Fast Response Shock
PTSD (Rest and Digest)	Invalidated Slow Response Shock

Notice that the labels displayed on the left correspond to the causes of disorders displayed on the right. And while this compares labels of a subjective origin with disorders of an objective origin (Frances, 2013b, p. 111-2), this end result identifies all the outcomes behind the established definition provided. This means that any proposed disorder cannot be currently added or removed. On top of this, the disorders are not allowed to be grouped, as the relationships represented between two occurrences are what constitutes two separate mental disorders. For the labels, however, these are subject to change given a new agreed upon label. But if, in any case, a mental disorder happens to have no proposed label, it will then be considered unrecognized by default.

This listing intends to serve as a template when identifying a mental disorder. It also allows for a baseline to create a more simplistic approach into how mental disorders can be categorized with respects to the given definition. This handbook commonly refers to this approach as the misplacement chart.

Based on the listing shown previously, repression and suppression are recognized to play a major role in the cause of various mental disorders. To illustrate this, a table was created to better categorize the various types that exist, while also incorporating the relationship each has with other types.

The chart shown on the right organizes twenty-six different mental disorders in a seven-cluster system, where each category would consist of two forms of that particular misplacement. The relationship between the two categories in the same cluster are known to be reciprocal, but if two categories are in two different clusters, then the relationship is to be considered unrelated. If the relationship between the two subtypes in the same category were considered, then they would simply serve as the same dimension.

CATEGORY

Cluster A: Guilt   Remorse

Cluster B: Paranoia   Special

Cluster C: Apathy   Worry

Cluster D: Envy   Jealousy

Cluster E: Anger   Fear

Cluster F: Arousal   Boredom

Cluster G: Psychological Shock

The overlaps section, which corresponds to the category section, establishes the comorbidity there is for the various mental disorders provided. Each number indicates what's undone in each category when the onset of the disorder occurs (1: identified category, 2: moral decision, 3: inconsistent model). And since what undoes the disorder is also reflective on the onset variation used, the onset prevents another disorder from overlapping if the way of undoing a category has the same onset variation.

Overlaps

1 | 1

2, 3 | 1, 2, 3

1 | 1

1 | 1

1 | 1

2 | 1, 2

3*

This concept of comorbidity is discussed more in depth in Section 6.1, but let's transition back to the chart displayed. Notice that the digit in place of psychological shock has an asterisk. This is to indicate that the represented category does not occur alongside the concept of misplacement, but rather through the sole use of the given onset variation, which in this case uses an inconsistent model. This is discussed further in Section 5.1 of this handbook.

1.4 THE CONCEPT OF MISPLACEMENT

For the other twelve categories that are given, the concept of misplacement plays an important role in how a mental disorder onsets in a given individual. In regards to this onset, the two forms differ with the concept of repression and suppression. What's required to onset misplacement demands that the individual struggles to cope with a specified category to the point of depression, and to incorporate the required onset variation(s) from the overlaps section when misplacement occurs. The specification, when admitting defeat in a depressive state, is that the individual could become in denial of that category (indicating repression) or become in denial of dealing with that category (indicating suppression). In order to prevent the onset of misplacement, the individual must be able to value (or correctly cope with) that category.

Note though, that in regards to individuals who are mentally ill, the onset variation is represented in the functionality of the given disorder, not in that of the individual. Such a misplacement, or impairment rather, cannot be understood through oneself or other individuals. As this consequence, in becoming mentally ill, leads to the inability for the individual to use the impaired category, as a result of onset.

Section 2: Emotions

When the onset of misplacement occurs for an emotion, the category that's involved becomes impaired, leaving the individual without the knowledge of that category. This situation results with a change in the individual, where the difference depends on what was misplaced, as an outcome of the given onset:

Misplaced Category: The concept serving as the misplacement becomes what's devalued, while the concept serving as the reciprocal becomes what's valued.

Misplaced Emotion: The individual would either represent an avoidance model if the emotion was repressed or represent an engagement model if the emotion was suppressed.

In using an example to better clarify this, let's take the category guilt from the misplacement chart and let's assume that it was repressed. Now, because this would indicate a misplaced category, the category guilt would be considered devalued by that individual. This means that the reciprocal of guilt, which is remorse (shown to the right of guilt), becomes what's valued. This is otherwise known as a consequence in the model (or representation of the disorder) that is reflected onto that of the individual. And since guilt, in this case, would represent a repressed emotion, the disorder uses an avoidance model, as a result of onset.

CATEGORY

Cluster A:	Guilt	Remorse
Cluster B:	Paranoia	Special
Cluster C:	Apathy	Worry
Cluster D:	Envy	Jealousy
Cluster E:	Anger	Fear
Cluster F:	Arousal	Boredom
Cluster G:	Psychological Shock	

Based on the model, there are specific triggers that correlate with the model itself. For example, in an avoidance model, the individual would seek to invalidate the external use of the misplacement by using the emotion's reciprocal. But as for an engagement model, the individual would seek to validate the external use of the misplacement by engaging in the emotion itself, where the subconscious would include a simulation in that of the reciprocal. However, if the use of the emotion is directed to either model, then the individual would seek to devalue the use of that emotion. Notice though, that these triggers are done uncontrollably, indicating that the triggers resemble features in the model, instead of being part of the individual.

Besides this, these models also deal with the concept of a boundary, or the selection of the misplacement. This boundary can entail the use of anger, which also represents the restriction in any given model. However, psychological pain would occur if the misplacement isn't viewed as a restriction. The exception here, is when psychological pain has numbed, as this evokes the experience of a brain zap instead (Warner CH, Bobo, Warner C, Reid, & Rachal; 2006; p. 449-56).

Coming back to the subconscious state though, this serves to manifest the misplacement in the model itself. For example, this can involve the appearance of an emotion, like fear, where the use of anger would be expressed instead (i.e. hostility resembled as a perceived threat).

Moving forward, the next idea that needs to be mentioned is the involvement of relationships. By comparing repressed guilt with other models of emotions, five different types of relationships can be identified. Examples of these relationship types are shown as follows:

Repressed Guilt + Suppressed Guilt: The relationship between these two types are opposites. Since both act to decrease the intensity of each other's model, these two form a close relationship, where the use of envy is purely positive, but changes when this type of envy is no longer directed in that relationship.

Repressed Guilt + Repressed Remorse: The relationship between these two types are reciprocal. Since both act to increase the intensity of each other's model, these two form a distant relationship, where the use of envy is purely negative, but changes when this type of envy is no longer directed in that relationship.

Repressed Guilt + Suppressed Remorse: The relationship between these two types are opposite and reciprocal. Since both don't act to either increase or decrease the intensity of each other's model, these two form an indifferent relationship, where the use of envy is not directed in that relationship.

Repressed Guilt + Repressed Guilt: The relationship between these two types are similar. Since one decreases, while the other increases the intensity of the other's model, these two form a one-directional relationship, where the negative use of envy is dependent on the model represented, and changes when envy is no longer directed in that relationship.

Repressed Guilt + Repressed Apathy: The relationship between these two types are unrelated. Since both have the possibility to either increase or decrease the intensity of each other's model, these two form an undetermined relationship, where the use of envy would be based on external factors, and changes when envy is no longer directed in that relationship.

These five relationship examples illustrate how a specific relationship plays out and intends to provide the predetermined relationship for any two particular models. They are also considered to be universal for every cluster, despite the fact that the main example used in each relationship is repressed guilt.

In regards to other points mentioned in the examples, however, envy serves as an extension, meaning that the models can still apply even without this addition. But as for the concept of intensity, decreasing intensity refers to the concept of satisfaction, while increasing intensity refers to the concept of dissatisfaction. With this in mind, dissatisfaction occurs when the individual has failed in expressing their own model. In turn, satisfaction implies that the model is openly expressed, where the cause would specify how the model is satisfied (Biere, 2009, p. 3-5).

2.4 TREATMENT GUIDELINES

Now, this fixed concept of satisfaction can influence the experience of a disorder for an individual, but isn't the underlining mechanism that undoes the impairment. According to Section 1.3, it was noted that the onset variation required for a misplaced emotion is an identified category. Because of this, treatment would be in regards to leading the individual to identifying that emotion, such that, the category would no longer remain impaired, which is provided below:

Internal Assistance: Identify the valued emotion that would appear to resemble an impulsive trigger, then question the behavior that occurs from those triggers. If gaps in memory [subconscious] are involved, attempt to recall where the source of this instance came from. Self-reflection can help identify the original category.

External Assistance: Determine whether the represented model is either an avoidance model or engagement model. Then, substitute an "I" statement during any model trigger that correctly justifies the usage of the misplaced emotion. This is done correctly only when another model trigger doesn't directly proceed that assertion. In doing this, the given trigger would be removed from the model, resulting in the individual's viewpoint of the valued emotion to be slightly altered.

If it helps to know the definitions behind the various emotions, this can be viewed in Section 6.3 of this handbook. In addition to this, another important note, which should be considered during the treatment process, is to never imply or even mention what the underlining category is to the individual. When it comes to all individuals on the mental disorder listing, hitting along a boundary that is reflective of an impairment in the individual is not to be tolerated.

Section 3: Memory Systems

3.1 CLUSTER B INTRO [DISSOCIATIVE DISORDERS]

When referring to a misplaced memory system, the individual is said to have a dissociative disorder due to meeting certain criteria. But before getting into what that criteria entails, let's first look at the two memory systems that exist and the differences there are between them:

Paranoia: [Memory System Not Specified]	Special: Autobiographical Memory System
Includes Information Gathered from an External Origin	Includes Information Gathered from an Internal Origin
Constructed Through [Not Specified]	Constructed Through a Personal Knowledge Base and Includes Visual Perspectives
Influenced By the Emotions: Remorse, Worry, Envy, and Fear	Influenced By the Emotions: Guilt, Apathy, Jealousy, and Anger
Derives Enjoyment through Something Meaningful	Derives Enjoyment through Oneself
Statements Include: "I can't be myself. I don't have emotions."	Statements Include: "I can be myself. I have emotions."

As shown above, these two categories serve to resemble a single memory system. The main difference between the two heavily relies on where the information was originally gathered from. In other words, the external origin refers to the information gathered from the surroundings of the self, while the internal origin refers to the information gathered from the self.

In addition to this, notice that the autobiographical memory system is constructed through something called a personal knowledge base. This information is indeed regarded as subjective, and serves as a use to store, formalize, and later recall personal knowledge within the self; similarly with the objectively-based memory system (Davies, Velez-

Morales, & King; 2005; p. 4-9). However, this is in contrast with the objectively-based memory system, in that it represents interpretations of factual information, as opposed to being comprised of factually-based information.

When formalizing a single memory from the knowledge base, this is referred to as a statement. Any statement from a particular memory system can be influenced by a specific emotion. This is because the axis that serves to represent the memory system is the same for the emotion it's influenced by. For example, if the emotion anger was to occur, then any statement that's influenced by that emotion will always use the autobiographical memory system.

The last aspect that's necessary to discuss in the table, is the concept of derived enjoyment. This is considered to be a resulting byproduct founded upon a given memory system, meaning that if a memory system were to become impaired, the same would be true for the derived enjoyment associated with it. As a result of this addition, laughter is allowed to occur as an outcome of combining derived enjoyment from a memory system with the breathing aspect from the respiratory system (Pocock & Richards, 2006, p. 315-7).

3.2 UNIVERSAL CRITERIA

Now, coming back to the criteria involved in a dissociative disorder, there are five indicators that coincide with its given classification. According to the individuals who've experienced a dissociative disorder, their experience illustrated is not by any means subjective, but would actually serve as what's universal when misplacing a memory system. This criteria, which was assembled by those individuals, is shown below:

1. There is a physical detachment from one's self, resulting in the ability to view the world in a subconscious state. *"You feel as though you're an onlooker, watching yourself live out life like a character in your own little movie."*
2. The perceived imagery of the world is projected as virtual rather than real. *"It's as if you're seeing the world through an entirely different lens."*

3. There is a more intense focus on the present, where the time standard fluctuates more severely based on the notion of how time is passing. *"It can feel as though you're stuck in time, being the only one aging typically."*
4. Experiences of stress levels are unusually higher than expected, resulting in the possibility of delusional beliefs. *"It would seem as if your judgement is clouded, only to be absorbed by a deceiving concept."*
5. The identity represents a single system of logic, where the disruption of memory co-exists. This is resembled in an unstable identity, with the inclusion of impulsivity through communication. *"It's as if you're taking control of yourself, where that person in control isn't you."*

Since one of the onset variations that's used happens to be an inconsistent model, the physical detachment from one's self occurs in order to satisfy this onset variation. As a result, the perceived imagery becomes virtual as a consequence of the physical detachment from one's self (Knight, 2002, p. 276-8). However, when it comes to the time standard fluctuations and the stress aspect involved, these have to do with the individual's perceived experience when functioning on a single memory system.

As for the last point given, this refers to the underlining differences between the four dissociative disorders, where impulsivity would occur as a representation of the disorder's functionality. This functionality, where the cause of the disorder and the system of logic is shown on the left and right respectively, is compared below:

Repressed Paranoia	Pointwise Circumscription
Suppressed Paranoia	Predicate Circumscription
Repressed Special	Closed-World Assumption
Suppressed Special	Open-World Assumption

When it comes to the individual's experience with the disorder, the physical detachment from one's self would allow for the ability to have awareness of that misplacement, in order for the individual's entire belief system to change as a result. Because of this, their belief would represent the axis that co-exists with that misplacement, where the horizontal line would serve as the category paranoia, while the vertical line would serve as the category special.

3.3 IDENTITY ANALYSIS IN WORLD ASSUMPTIONS

Since their belief would represent what the individual misplaced, pushing away from this is done by the formalization in the identity itself. This formalization, in regards to the open-world assumption and closed-world assumption respectively, is provided below from its given Wikipedia page:

In a formal system of logic used for knowledge representation, the **open-world assumption** is the assumption that the truth value of a statement may be true irrespective of whether or not it is known to be true. It is the opposite of the closed-world assumption, which holds that any statement that is true is also known to be true.

The open-world assumption (OWA) codifies the informal notion that in general no single agent or observer has complete knowledge, and therefore cannot make the closed-world assumption. The OWA limits the kinds of inference and deductions an agent can make to those that follow from statements that are known to the agent to be true. In contrast, the closed world assumption allows an agent to infer, from its lack of knowledge of a statement being true, anything that follows from that statement being false.

Heuristically, the open-world assumption applies when we represent knowledge within a system as we discover it, and where we cannot guarantee that we have discovered or will discover complete information. In the OWA, statements about knowledge that are not included in or inferred from the knowledge explicitly recorded in the system may be considered unknown, rather than wrong or false.

Semantic Web languages such as OWL make the open-world assumption. The absence of a particular statement within the web means, in principle, that the statement has not been made explicitly yet, irrespective of whether it would be true or not, and irrespective of whether we believe that it would be true or not. In essence, from the absence of a statement alone, a deductive reasoner cannot (and must not) infer that the statement is false.

Many procedural programming languages and databases make the closed-world assumption. For example, if a typical airline database does not contain a seat assignment for a traveler, it is assumed that the traveler has not checked in. The closed-world assumption typically applies when a system has complete control over information; this is the case with many database applications where the database transaction system acts as a central broker and arbiter of concurrent requests by multiple independent clients (e.g., airline booking agents). There are, however, many databases with incomplete information: for example, one cannot assume that because there is no mention on a patient's history of a particular allergy that the patient does not suffer from that allergy.

Example:

Statement: "Mary" "is a citizen of" "France"

Question: Is Paul a citizen of France?

"Closed world" (for example SQL) answer: No.

"Open world" answer: Unknown.

Under OWA, failure to derive a fact does not imply the opposite. For example, assume we only know that Mary is a citizen of France. From this information we can neither conclude that Paul is not a citizen of France, nor that he is. Therefore, we admit the fact that our knowledge of the world is incomplete. The open-world assumption is closely related to the monotonic nature of first-order logic: adding new information never falsifies a previous conclusion. Namely, if we subsequently learn that Paul is also a citizen of France, this does not change any earlier positive or negative conclusions.

The language of logic programs with strong negation allows us to postulate the closed-world assumption for some predicates and leave the other predicates in the realm of the open-world assumption.[1]

[1] Strong negation refers to the representation of incomplete information (Russell & Norvig, 2010).

The **closed-world assumption** (CWA), in a formal system of logic used for knowledge representation, is the presumption that a statement that is true is also known to be true. Therefore, conversely, what is not currently known to be true, is false. The same name also refers to a logical formalization of this assumption by Raymond Reiter.[1] The opposite of the closed-world assumption is the open-world assumption (OWA), stating that lack of knowledge does not imply falsity. Decisions on CWA vs. OWA determine the understanding of the actual semantics of a conceptual expression with the same notations of concepts. A successful formalization of natural language semantics usually cannot avoid an explicit revelation of whether the implicit logical backgrounds are based on CWA or OWA.

Negation as failure is related to the closed-world assumption, as it amounts to believing false every predicate that cannot be proved to be true.

In the context of knowledge management, the closed-world assumption is used in at least two situations: (1) when the knowledge base is known to be complete (e.g., a corporate database containing records for every employee), and (2) when the knowledge base is known to be incomplete but a "best" definite answer must be derived from incomplete information. For example, if a database contains the following table reporting editors who have worked on a given article, a query on the people not having edited the article on Formal Logic is usually expected to return "Sarah Johnson".

Edit	
Editor	**Article**
John Doe	Formal Logic
Joshua A. Norton	Formal Logic
Sarah Johnson	Introduction to Spatial Databases
Charles Ponzi	Formal Logic
Emma Lee-Choon	Formal Logic

In the closed-world assumption, the table is assumed to be complete (it lists all editor-article relationships), and Sarah Johnson is the only editor who has not edited the article on Formal Logic.

[1] (Gallaire & Minker, 1978, p. 119-40).

The Mental Illness Handbook

In contrast, with the open-world assumption the table is not assumed to contain all editor-article tuples, and the answer to who has not edited the Formal Logic article is unknown. There is an unknown number of editors not listed in the table, and an unknown number of articles edited by Sarah Johnson that are also not listed in the table.

The first formalization of the closed-world assumption in formal logic consists in adding to the knowledge base the negation of the literals that are not currently entailed by it. The result of this addition is always consistent if the knowledge base is in Horn form, but is not guaranteed to be consistent otherwise. For example, the knowledge base

{English(Fred) ∨ Irish(Fred)}

Entails neither **{English(Fred)** nor **Irish(Fred)}**

Adding the negation of these two literals to the knowledge base leads to

{English(Fred) ∨ Irish(Fred)}, ¬{English(Fred) ∨ ¬Irish(Fred)}

which is inconsistent. In other words, this formalization of the closed-world assumption sometimes turns a consistent knowledge base into an inconsistent one. The closed-world assumption does not introduce an inconsistency on a knowledge base **K** exactly when the intersection of all Herbrand models of **K** is also a model of **K**; in the propositional case, this condition is equivalent to **K** having a single minimal model, where a model is minimal if no other model has a subset of variables assigned to true.

3.4 IDENTITY ANALYSIS IN CIRCUMSCRIPTION

Besides the functionality of the open-world assumption and closed-world assumption, as mentioned above, there is still the functionality of circumscription that has yet to be discussed. But before doing so, one aspect that's worth mentioning is that the term predicate, when used in the context of a memory system, differs from a statement in that it asserts something about the subject (Cunningham, 2012, p. 29). With this in mind, circumscription is provided as follows from its given Wikipedia page (with predicate circumscription and pointwise circumscription in that order):

Circumscription is a non-monotonic logic created by John McCarthy to formalize the common sense assumption that things are as expected unless otherwise specified.[1,2] To implement circumscription in its initial formulation, McCarthy augmented first-order logic to allow the minimization of the extension of some predicates, where the extension of a predicate is the set of tuples of values the predicate is true on. This minimization is similar to the closed-world assumption that what is not known to be true is false.[3]

The original definition of circumscription proposed by McCarthy is about first-order logic. The role of variables in propositional logic (something that can be true or false) is played in first-order logic by predicates. Namely, a propositional formula can be expressed in first-order logic by replacing each propositional variable with a predicate of zero arity (i.e., a predicate with no arguments). Therefore, minimization is done on predicates in the first-order logic version of circumscription: the circumscription of a formula is obtained forcing predicates to be false whenever possible.[4]

Given a first-order logic formula T containing a predicate P circumscribing this predicate amounts to selecting only the models of T in which P is assigned to true on a minimal set of tuples of values.

Formally, the extension of a predicate in a first-order model is the set of tuples of values this predicate assign to true in the model. First-order models indeed includes the evaluation of each predicate symbol; such an evaluation tells whether the predicate is true or false for any possible value of its arguments.[5] Since each argument of a predicate must be a term, and each term evaluates to a value, the models tells whether $P(v_1, \ldots, v_n)$ is true for any possible tuple of values $\langle v_1, \ldots, v_n \rangle$. The extension of P in a model is the set of tuples of terms such that $P(v_1 \ldots, v_n)$ is true in the model.

The circumscription of a predicate P in a formula T is obtained by selecting only the models of T with a minimal extension of P. For example, if a formula has only two models, differing only because $P(v_1, \ldots, v_n)$ is true in one and false in the second, then only the second model is selected. This is because $\langle v_1 \ldots, v_n \rangle$ is in the extension of P in the first model but not in the second.

[1] (McCarthy, 1986, p. 89-116)
[2] (McCarthy, 1980, p. 27-39)
[3] (Eiter & Gottlab, 1993, p. 231-45)
[4] (Gabbay, Hogger, & Robinson; 1998; p. 297-352)
[5] (Cadoli, 1992, p. 113-8)

This definition only allows circumscribing a single predicate. While the extension to more than one predicate is trivial, minimizing the extension of a single predicate has an important application: capturing the idea that things are usually as expected. This idea can be formalized by minimizing a single predicate expressing the abnormality of situations. In particular, every known fact is expressed in logic with the addition of a literal ¬**Abnormal(...)** stating that the fact holds only in normal situations. Minimizing the extension of this predicate allows for reasoning under the implicit assumption that things are as expected (that is, they are not abnormal), and that this assumption is made only if possible (abnormality can be assumed false only if this is consistent with the facts.)

Pointwise circumscription is a variant of first-order circumscription that has been introduced by Vladimir Lifschitz.[1] In the propositional case, pointwise and predicate circumscription coincide. The rationale of pointwise circumscription is that it minimizes the value of a predicate for each tuple of values separately, rather than minimizing the extension of the predicate. For example, there are two models of $P(a) \equiv P(b)$ with domain $\{a, b\}$, one setting $P(a) = P(b) = false$ and the other setting $P(a) = P(b) = true$. Since the extension of P in the first model is $\emptyset$ while the extension for the second is $\{a, b\}$, circumscription only selects the first model.

In pointwise circumscription, each tuple of values is considered separately. For example, in the formula $P(a) \equiv P(b)$ one would consider the value of $P(a)$ separately from $P(b)$. A model is minimal only if it is not possible to turn any such value from true to false while still satisfying the formula. As a result, the model in which $P(a) = P(b) = true$ is selected by pointwise circumscription because turning only $P(a)$ into false does not satisfy the formula, and the same happens for $P(b)$.

Notice that, in regards to circumscription, there are two truth value settings. One of the truth value settings, which is false, acts as a continuation to the truth value setting that is true. Something similar was discussed back in Section 2.2, about how the subconscious state serves to represent the misplacement in the model itself and to contain a simulation in that of the reciprocal.

[1] (Lifschitz, 1986, p. 406-10)

This means that, in respects to the systems of logic that were previously mentioned, the subconscious state is represented as the truth value of a false statement or predicate, where the functionality for both types of circumscription would contain a false predicate. This is contrary to the two world assumptions, where no false statement can exist. The reason for this, has to do with the functionality being based on the formalization of the memory system presented, instead of being on the misplacement. This is discussed further in Section 4.2 of this handbook.

3.5 TREATMENT GUIDELINES

Now, the other aspect that's influenced by the memory system's functionality is the treatment requirement that involved. When it comes to the onset variations used, both memory systems would use a moral decision, while only one memory system would also include an identified category. Because of this, there are slight alterations that go along with the treatment of each model, as a result of using a moral decision, which is shown below:

Pointwise Circumscription (Repressed, X-axis): Requires a decision to accept the x-axis, serving to represent part of the individual.

Predicate Circumscription (Suppressed, X-axis): Requires a decision to deal with the x-axis, serving to represent part of the individual.

Closed-World Assumption (Repressed, Y-axis): Requires a decision to substitute and accept the y-axis, serving to represent part of the individual.

Open-World Assumption (Suppressed, Y-axis): Requires a decision to substitute and deal with the y-axis, serving to represent part of the individual.

In dissociative disorders, the moral decision is represented through the use of memory. This is why the decision as to whether the individual wants to get out of the disorder is left upon that of the individual. However, if the individual decides to stay with the disorder, slight progress can be made for those who struggle with the y-axis, but only if personal information gathered externally is recognized as the self. Assistance is involved in allowing for control, discerning personal beliefs, validating decision making, and note-taking. The same holds true for x-axis types, but the only difference is that the assistance in decisions isn't included.

Realize though, that the use of the unimpaired memory system is required in order for treatment to work. For example, suppose that the current method in treating a y-axis type involves discerning personal beliefs. The closed-world assumption can express a want in such a way that allows another individual to formalize an "I" statement, serving as an assertion for the closed-world assumption. However, it must be the case that this formalization is done through the use of the factually-based memory system, otherwise, any possible assistance here would not be given. This is contrary to that of the open-world assumption, where the formalization would be done by the individual with the disorder, instead of, the individual giving external assistance.

Section 4: States of Being

4.1 CLUSTER F INTRO [PSYCHIATRIC DISORDERS]

Remember when we brought up the individual's experience with misplacing a memory system, and said that what they misplaced served as the axis that represents their belief system. Well, just like how there is a fixed dimension with a given memory system, the same also happens to be true with that of the entire listing.

In order to illustrate this on the misplacement chart shown on the right, this handbook will indicate the x-axis with the use of an apostrophe and the y-axis with the use of a quotation mark. But as for knowing which fixed dimension goes with each category, remember that if the given category can occur from an external origin, then it would represent an x-axis. And if the given category can occur from an internal origin, then it would represent a y-axis. Notice though, that this may not always be true for every cluster. Suppose that there is only one category in a particular cluster. This would result in the category to be represented as an x-axis by default.

CATEGORY

Cluster A: Guilt"   Remorse'

Cluster B: Paranoia'   Special"

Cluster C: Apathy"   Worry'

Cluster D: Envy'   Jealousy"

Cluster E: Anger"   Fear'

Cluster F: Arousal'   Boredom"

Cluster G: Psychological Shock'

4.2 MODEL FUNCTIONS

However, this concept allows us to determine the dimension for a given category, not the functionality of a given model. For example, the category arousal uses the concept of an interest, which can be gathered from an external origin. This gives the argument that the category would serve as that of the x-axis, but no insight as to what the functionality (or definition) of repressed arousal would look like. As a result, a concept that's used to explain this information is known as the y-axis evaluation (Friedberg, Insel, & Spence; 2003; p. 48-9).

The y-axis evaluation determines whether its functionality has a relation with that of the reciprocal. Based on this evaluation, the y-axis would also provide the relation type (dependent or independent) to that of the x-axis. This determines the model function that is used for a single cluster. For example,

	X-axis	Y-axis
R:	Y	X
S:	$s(X) + Y$	$s(Y) + X$

Notice that the letters "R" and "S" indicate repression and suppression respectively, while "s(X)" would denote as the subconscious state of the given axis in parentheses. This model function is used whenever the y-axis has an independent relation in respects to the x-axis. An independent relation type would give the indication that this is a misplacement-based functionality, where the difference between "R" and "S" would imply how the misplacement is used in the given model.

	X-axis	Y-axis
R:	$s(X) + -Y$	$-X$
S:	$s(X) + Y$	X

In this example, "-X" refers to the opposite function of "X". This is unlike the previous model function in that the y-axis has a dependent relation in respects to the x-axis. A dependent relation type would indicate that this is a reciprocal-based functionality, where the difference between "R" and "S" would imply how the functionality of the reciprocal is used in the given model.

Notice though, that the second model function must have the x-axis represented in every model, but only because the functionality of the y-axis depends on the x-axis being represented. A similar situation would occur if the x-axis evaluation had a dependent relation type over the y-axis, as the difference would make for the placements of the x-axis and y-axis switched, as a result. However, since the y-axis evaluation can express all the models that use the concept of misplacement, this makes the use of the x-axis evaluation nonessential.

In some instances though, the relation type dictates the onset variation used for the models selected. For example, an identified category is presented in every model where the formalized category is influenced by an independent axis type, while a moral decision is presented in every model where the formalized category is influenced by a dependent axis type. However, some cases, like with an inconsistent model, have no specified relation type, implying that an evaluation cannot determine the functionality of a category that solely uses an inconsistent model.

4.3 FORMALIZING AROUSAL

But unlike the functionality of the emotions, which makes the first model function, the functionality of the states of being, similarly to that of the memory systems, makes the second model function. However, when it comes to the differences between the memory systems and states of being, the formalization of the models are instead done by the opposing function, where some of the terms originally given are replaced to appropriately suit the functionality of a state of being. In the case of misplaced boredom, the functionality of arousal [X] and its opposite [-X] are respectively shown as expected:

S: *"A known interest is presumed to be engaged in, therefore, what is known to not be an interest is presumed not to be engaged in."*

This model holds that interests are to be fixed, complete, and represented under a single interpretation, where an interest can be opposed until otherwise engaged in. This model allows another to decide whether or not an interest should be engaged in, anything that follows from that being opposed, as the model can't allow an engaged interest to be unknown.

R: *"The decision of an interest is assumed to be engaged in, regardless of whether that interest is also known to be engaged in."*

In this model, interests are to be expandable, incomplete, and represented under multiple interpretations, where an interest can be engaged in until otherwise opposed. It limits the suggestions another can make to only those that follow from interests that are known to be engaged in, as the model can't allow an engaged interest to be opposed.

4.4 FORMALIZING BOREDOM

As for the functionality of boredom [Y], it *maximizes the sequence of decisions a predicate of an interest is assigned to engage in,* while the opposite [-Y] *maximizes the decision of a predicate of an interest for each sequence of decisions separately.* Consequently, both functions seek to minimize the functionality of their known opposite. For instance,

R: Predicate $(d_1, \_\_, d_x)$ = Engage $\oplus^1$ Oppose

This model restricts the predicate of an interest, forcing it to be opposed whenever possible. Doing so restricts the selection of the model where a predicate is assigned to engage in on a given sequence of decisions. An evaluation decides whether a predicate should be engaged in for any possible decisions of its argument. Each argument of a predicate must evaluate to a decision, telling whether a predicate should be engaged in for any possible sequence of decisions. The model can engage in a single predicate only when the selected predicate can't be opposed. As a result, the model ends when an engaged predicate happens to be unknown.

S: Predicate A $\leftrightarrow^2$ Predicate B   {A, B} = Engage

In this model, there are two distinct settings with a given domain {A, B}. Since the extension of a predicate in the first setting is an empty set,

---

[1] The exclusive disjunction, otherwise known as "$\oplus$", refers to the concept of "either A or B, but not, A and B" (Simpson, 1987, p. 550-4).

[2] The logical biconditional, or "$\leftrightarrow$", refers to the concept of "A if and only if B" (Hurley, 2014, p. 317).

while the extension of the second is to be engaged in, the model restricts the selection of the first setting. This model considers each sequence of decisions separately, as predicate A is thought to be different from predicate B. The model is minimal only if it's not possible to turn any decision from being engaged in, to not being engaged in, while still satisfying the model. As a result, engaging in both predicates is what's selected, as the model ends when an engaged predicate happens to be opposed.

4.5 TREATMENT GUIDELINES

This concept behind ending the model is referring to when the individual would feel boredom in their disorder. However, the model would end if it's formalized by boredom, but not arousal. This is because, in any model-based functionality, a model that's formalized from a dependent axis type doesn't require an identified category in treatment. Instead, the axis type serves as the moral decision that undoes the model. And since its boredom, these four models can be modified by external factors, including the use of certain substances, like medication (Raffa & Porreca, 1989, p. 245-58). This is indeed useful for models that are unstable, and why the term psychiatric serves as the classification for these four mental disorders.

Now, in regards to the two models that require an identified category, ending either model would only lead to psychological pain, and would require a moral decision prior to self-reflection being considered. But just like in that of the memory systems, treating a model can be done through the use of its known opposite, as the opposite serves the function of satisfying that model.

For example, assisting "R" in the formalization of boredom would require using the functionality of "S" in treatment. This is done only when necessary, resulting in the functionality of "R" to not be allowed to oppose the single predicate selected, and thus leading to the end of the model if enough predicates are decided to be engaged in. This is in contrast with that of the memory systems, where the formalization of the logical biconditional isn't used.

Section 5: Mental Shock

One aspect that should be noted, in regards to the last cluster, is that the concept of either repression or suppression isn't used to onset misplacement. The reason for this, has to do with what was mentioned back in Section 2.1, about how satisfying a misplaced category would require there to be an effect on the reciprocal. But since there happens to be no defined reciprocal to psychological shock, the concept of misplacement ends up not being used, as a result.

What does come into play, however, is the onset variation that is used for the given category. And since the category happens to use an inconsistent model as its onset variation, this would play an important role in how the category can become impaired. In addition to this, Section 4.3 gave the indication that the functionality of arousal [X] makes the closed-world assumption. Interestingly enough, applying this functionality to that of psychological shock will determine the function of that category in its respected cluster.

For example, because the last cluster on the right does not contain a y-axis, this leads to no determined relation type for that of the x-axis. However, by using the closed-world assumption, failing to have a category represented as the y-axis leads to a "consistent" model: *"shock reaction = unexpected memory stimuli"*. This model sets up the onset variation that is used with that of the memory systems. And since there are only two types of

CATEGORY

Cluster A: Guilt"   Remorse'

Cluster B: Paranoia'   Special"

Cluster C: Apathy"   Worry'

Cluster D: Envy'   Jealousy"

Cluster E: Anger"   Fear'

Cluster F: Arousal'   Boredom"

Cluster G: Psychological Shock'

memory systems involved, this would mean that there also exists two types of shock reactions as an outcome. However, this arises an issue, because the ability to invalidate (or take the reciprocal of) a memory system does not hold the same for that of a shock reaction, as this trigger would cause the "consistent" model to become undefined.

In order for the model to become undefined, the invalidated memory must contradict the memory used to invalidate it. However, this must be the case during the occurrence of a shock reaction, as the model cannot become inconsistent otherwise. For example, assume that a book plummeted from the shelf onto the floor, a shock reaction would result if the sound that was exerted from the book was unexpected. An observer could contradict this occurrence, however, by arguing that no shelf was built for the book to be placed on.

This makes for an inconsistent model, as the information gathered from an internal origin invalidates the information gathered from an external origin. Besides this, it should be noted that the invalidated memory is allowed to originate from either memory system. For example, in the case that the invalidated memory uses information gathered from an internal origin, a different type of shock reaction would occur contrary from the one in the example. But since the represented cluster is only one-dimensional, the relationship between the two types of shock are opposite rather than reciprocal. These two settings at which shock can be experienced are shown as follows:

Fast Response Shock (Blackout): connects with memory gathered externally; increased respiratory rate and heart rate (fight or flight type).

Slow Response Shock (Blackout): connects with memory gathered internally; decreased respiratory rate and heart rate (rest and digest type).

This is indicative of two separate disorders, as the relationship between the two types of shock are considered to be opposite. In this sense, making this argument would mean that any disorder represented is dependent on the type of shock reaction used in the model. This is justified with two aspects: 1) that the two disorders differ with the type of memory system that it's connected with (internal or external origin), and 2) that the two disorders differ with the given shock response regarding respiratory rate and heart rate (increased or decreased). This handbook separates these two disorders by denoting them as either the fight or flight type or the rest and digest type, which is in respects similar to the two opposing functions of the autonomic nervous system (Brodal, 2004, p. 369–96).

Notice though, that these two disorders share the concept of a blackout trigger. This is because the blackout intends to represent the undefined memory in the model. With this in mind, the blackout trigger would result simply from the impairment of both the single shock setting and the given invalidated memory, where the boundary would represent the type of shock setting that's restricted in the model. This leaves the individual with the inability to put into concept what the situation entailed, and that invalidating any memory that's connected with the boundary is what satisfies the model.

5.3 RE-EXPERIENCING EVENT

In regards to the duration of the mental shock model, the blackout would re-emerge in situations where the individual would recognize the formalization of the invalidated memory from its affected origin (internal or external). However, this concept, when involving the trigger, does not give recollection of the invalidated memory, but instead, leaves the memory undefined. Note though, that this blackout is represented unconsciously rather than subconsciously. This is due to the fact that the visual system is deactivated in this process, rather than the auditory system (Szeliski, 2010, p. 3-16) (Beigi, 2011, p. 75-141).

One thing that should be noted though, is that this trigger does not occur when the individual is faced with a physical detail of the invalidated memory. In fact, this situation would lead the individual to unknowingly avoid any resemblance of that memory, while also believing in the reciprocal memory, because it satisfies the onset. This concept is indeed similar to what was mentioned back in Section 2.1, about how satisfying the onset meant that a single concept had to be valued, while its reciprocal had to be devalued. In this context though, the invalidated memory and the reciprocal memory are devalued and valued respectively.

However, given an invalidated memory and a reciprocal memory, such interpretations of these memories can be expanded upon, such that, it is consistent with that of the reciprocal memory. In a certain interpretation, that is, the individual can be impacted negatively by the memory they believe in, possibly leading to nightmares in the fight or flight type, but not in the rest and digest type. This is because, in the fight or flight type, the reciprocal memory serves as the information gathered from an internal origin. And since the memory takes from the autobiographical memory system, this can be reflected in that of a visual perspective, where the content involved, even in regards to a nightmare, would be based on the personal belief of the individual.

5.4 TREATMENT GUIDELINES

This aspect regarding nightmares is disregarded when establishing the model. The reasoning here, is that the concept of nightmares simply extends from the model, as opposed to being part of the model. But besides this insignificance, the onset variation involved in treating these two disorders uses an inconsistent model. For this reason, creating an inconsistency in the model requires a certain realization to be made, such that, the reciprocal memory is no longer believed in.

It should be made clear though, that this realization (of undoing the model) cannot be done through the use of external assistance, as this onset variation prohibits such a notion being considered. And since this concept is also seen with that of the identified category and moral decision, this restriction only permits the individual the ability to undo the model.

However, in recalling that the given shock setting is also restricted in the model. This means that the circumstances, where unexpected memory stimuli occurs, is also restricted. These situations argue that such involvement should be minimized (i.e. loud noises, being touched, etc.). But since some cases can be unavoidable, this would entail satisfying the model in the event that the situation occurred.

Section 6: Additional Concepts

6.1 COMPONENTS INVOLVING OVERLAP

In the last section, it was stated that the inconsistent model uses the concept of a realization to not only undo, but to also satisfy the onset of that disorder. However, when it comes to the properties of onset variations, these serve as an important application when concerning the comorbidity for any specified model.

For example, suppose that the comparison is between repressed paranoia {2, 3} and the fight or flight type {3}. Since both involve an inconsistent model, while repressed paranoia also includes the aspect of a moral decision, these two models use the concept of a realization when undoing the model. This realization is otherwise known as a change in the individual's belief system, where what is believed in, in the case of the fight or flight type, is reflected by that of the reciprocal memory.

Overlaps

1 | 1

2, 3 | 1, 2, 3

1 | 1

1 | 1

1 | 1

2 | 1, 2

3*

Notice though, that this concept was discussed back in Section 3.2, about how the belief system for repressed paranoia would serve as that of the x-axis. However, in terms of comorbidity, when arguing that the fight or flight type follows from repressed paranoia, this is considered problematic. Since the inconsistent model has an involvement with memory, and because repressed paranoia is equivalent to that of an impaired memory system, this would lead the reciprocal memory to the inability of contradicting the impaired invalidated memory, resulting with the indication that the fight or flight type can't onset.

However, suppose that the comparison was between suppressed arousal {2} and the fight or flight type {3} instead. These two disorders can be comorbid, as suppressed arousal doesn't have any implication with memory. And since the fight or flight type purely uses an inconsistent model in order to onset, this would suggest that the only reason these two disorders are comorbid, is simply due to the lack of an inconsistent model in that of suppressed arousal. As a result, this leads to the reasoning that two models can't be comorbid if and only if both use the same onset variation.

This argument is also supported by what was mentioned back in Section 5.4, about how an onset variation holds a restriction in undoing the model through the use of external assistance. For instance, an individual with the rest and digest type {3} cannot also have the fight or flight type {3} represented, as the inconsistent model doesn't allow for a change in belief system through the use of external assistance. In principle, this property makes it such that the belief system would have to be undone in order for another change in belief system to occur.

6.2 ZERO-DIMENSIONAL CATEGORIES

In thinking more broadly, onset variations are formalized through the use of a given memory system, and fundamentally allow for mental disorders to exist. Furthermore, these are only represented in categories that serve as a single dimension. In other words, onset variations can only psychologically impair physical entities (categories depicting a single dimension), as opposed to non-physical entities (categories depicting a zeroth dimension) (Hazewinkel, 1989, p. 188-90).

But due to the nature of the provided definition, this handbook only displays physical entities on the misplacement chart. As such, entities in the case of psychological pain and stress are not established in a given cluster, suggesting that an impairment given would not indicate an abnormality. But in spite of both still representing a category, these still serve the function of a psychological concept regardless. With this in mind, zero-dimensional categories share two particular attributes:

1. The concept of degrees, otherwise denoted as a numerical value, is represented.
2. The occurrence of the category, in terms of the individual's viewpoint, is devalued.

Notice that the concept of degrees is not used in one-dimensional categories. This is because physical entities amount to the object itself, making the concept trivial. However, when it comes to non-physical entities in an individual, these amount from either external influences or complex internal processes (Ulrich-Lai & Herman, 2017, p. 397-409). In any case, zero-dimensional categories still consist of how the construct is viewed, with the feature of being devalued by default. But despite this, certain processes do allow for these categories to be valued.

But before getting into the psychological representations of these two categories, establishing the concepts with that of physical entities are needed if such concepts were to be described. That being said, zero-dimensional categories can be observed physically in an individual, rather than psychologically. For instance, *stress is created in a subject when it exerts a pushing force onto another subject or object inwardly,* whereas *pain is created in a subject when it exerts a pulling force onto another subject or object outwardly*. These concepts indeed function equivalently to the psychologically-represented zero-dimensional categories, where the difference would depend on the origin of the body part in question.

It should be noted though, that in regards to how a given category is viewed, zero-dimensional categories don't involve a consequence on the reciprocal. Apart from this, let's say that an individual was to direct stress onto a psychological facet of themselves. Since stress is denoted numerically, such a concept directed onto its origin would lead to a decrease in the amount of stress exerted. This valued concept would result in a deformation, otherwise referred to as a psychological adjustment in the individual. However, this end result is temporary if the amount of stress left over is not entirely depleted. Conversely, the depletion of stress levels would indicate a permanent effect, where psychological pain would substitute, as a result (Wu, 2005, p. 45-132).

Realize though, that the amount of stress reduced is marked by the amount of derived enjoyment obtained in the process. This byproduct, even with the inclusion of diminishing (or valuing) the amount of psychological pain presented, can be resolved by re-devaluing that category. Besides this, zero-dimensional categories can be expressed through the formalization of memory. This can be exemplified through the depletion of stress, where the formalization of the statement, "I changed" would lead to psychological pain. Incidentally, this concept is similar to what was mentioned back in Section 2.2, about how psychological pain can result upon misplacing a category.

However, speaking of a misplaced category, Section 1.2 stated that all the outcomes in what was defined as a mental disorder was identified, and that any proposed disorder couldn't be added or removed. This was termed "currently" though, as it assumes that the development for that of a human being can change with the inclusion of further implementations. But in terms of supporting this claim, this can be directed toward the emotions defined below:

Remorse - *allows for the ability to use and acknowledge the concept of culpability from an external origin.*

Guilt - *allows for the ability to use and acknowledge the concept of culpability from an internal origin.*

Worry - *allows for the ability to use and acknowledge the concept of uncertainty from an external origin.*

Apathy - *allows for the ability to use and acknowledge the concept of uncertainty from an internal origin.*

Envy - *allows for the ability to use and acknowledge the concept of desire from an external origin.*

Jealousy - *allows for the ability to use and acknowledge the concept of desire from an internal origin.*

Fear - *allows for the ability to use and acknowledge the concept of restriction from an external origin.*

Anger - *allows for the ability to use and acknowledge the concept of restriction from an internal origin.*

In theory, the concepts listed here (i.e. culpability, uncertainty, desire, etc.) can be expanded upon, implying that a modification in the misplacement chart would be necessary in order for new disorders to be established. However, since the current institution of individuals only acquire the provided eight emotions given above, extensions in an individual must be introduced prior to new installments being made.

References:

American Psychiatric Association (2000). "Diagnostic and statistical manual of mental disorders" (4th ed), Text Revision, DSM-IV-TR, Washington, DC: American Psychiatric Association.

Beigi, H. (2011). "Fundamentals of speaker recognition". New York: Springer Science & Business Media, LLC. pp. 75-141. ISBN 978-0-387-77591-3.

Biere, A. (2009). "Handbook of satisfiability". Amsterdam Washington, DC: IOS Press. pp. 3-5. ISBN 978-1-58-603929-5.

Brodal, P. (2004). "The central nervous system: Structure and Function" (3rd ed.). Oxford University Press US. pp. 369–96. ISBN 0-19-516560-8.

Cadoli, M. (1992). "The complexity of model checking for circumscriptive formulae". Information Processing Letters. 44 (3): pp. 113–8. doi:10.1016/0020-0190(92)90049-2.

Cunningham, D. W. (2012). "A logical introduction to proof". New York, NY: Springer. pp. 29. ISBN 978-1-46-143631-7.

Davies, S.; Velez-Morales, J.; & King, R. (2005). "Building the memex sixty years later: trends and directions in personal knowledge bases". Technical Report CU-CS-997-05. Boulder, Colorado: Department of Computer Science, University of Colorado at Boulder. pp. 4-9.

Eiter, T. & Gottlob, G. (1993). "Propositional circumscription and extended closed world reasoning are $\Pi P2$-complete". Theoretical Computer Science. 114 (2): pp. 231–45. doi:10.1016/0304-3975(93)90073-3.

Frances, A. (2013a). "The new crisis of confidence in psychiatric diagnosis". Annals of Internal Medicine. 159 (2): pp. 221–2. doi:10.7326/0003-4819-159-3-201308060-00655. PMID 23685989.

Frances, A. (2013b). "The past, present and future of psychiatric diagnosis". World Psychiatry. 12 (2): pp. 111–2. doi:10.1002/wps.20027. PMC 3683254 Freely accessible. PMID 23737411.

Friedberg, S.; Insel, A.; & Spence, L. (2003). "Linear algebra" (4th ed.). Upper Saddle River, N.J: Pearson Education. pp. 48–9. ISBN 978-0-13-008451-4.

Gabbay, D. M.; Hogger, C. J.; & Robinson, J. A. (1998). "Handbook of logic in artificial intelligence and logic programming". Oxford, New York: Clarendon Press Oxford University Press. pp. 297–352. ISBN 978-0-19-853747-2.

Gallaire, H. & Minker, J. (1978). "Logic and data bases". New York: Plenum Press. pp. 119–40. ISBN 978-0-30-640060-5.

Hazewinkel, M. (1989). "Encyclopaedia of mathematics". Dordrecht: Kluwer Academic Publishers. Vol. 3: pp. 188-90. ISBN 978-94-009-5994-1.

Hurley, P. (2014). "A concise introduction to logic" (12th ed.). Australia: Cengage Learning. pp. 317. ISBN 978-1-28-519654-1.

Knight, R. D. (2002). "Five easy lessons: strategies for successful physics teaching". San Francisco, California: Addison Wesley. pp. 276–8. ISBN 978-0-80-538702-5.

Lifschitz, V. (1986). "AAAI-86 proceedings of the fifth national conference on artificial intelligence", August 11-15, 1986, Philadelphia, Pa. Los Altos, California: Distributed by Morgan Kaufmann Publishers. pp. 406–10. ISBN 978-0-93-461313-2.

McCarthy, J. (1980). "Circumscription – A form of non-monotonic reasoning". Artificial Intelligence. 13: pp. 27–39. doi:10.1016/0004-3702(80)90011-9.

McCarthy, J. (1986). "Applications of circumscription to formalizing common-sense knowledge". Artificial Intelligence. 28 (1): pp. 89–116. doi:10.1016/0004-3702(86)90032-9.

Pocock, G. & Richards, C. D. (2006). "Human physiology: the basis of medicine" (3rd ed.). Oxford New York: Oxford University Press. pp. 315–7. ISBN 978-0-19-856878-0.

Raffa R. B. & Porreca F. (1989). "Thermodynamic analysis of the drug-receptor interaction". Life Sciences. 44 (4): pp. 245–58. doi:10.1016/0024-3205(89)90182-3. PMID 2536880.

Russell, S. J. & Norvig, P. (2010). "Artificial intelligence: a modern approach" (3rd ed.). Upper Saddle River, NJ: Prentice Hall. ISBN 978-0-13-604259-4.

Simpson, R. (1987). "Introductory electronics for scientists and engineers" (2nd ed.). Boston: Allyn and Bacon. pp. 550-4. ISBN 978-0-20-508377-0.

Szeliski, R. (2010). "Computer vision: algorithms and applications". Springer Science & Business Media. pp. 3–16. ISBN 978-1-84882-935-0.

The Mental Illness Handbook

Ulrich-Lai, Y. M. & Herman, J. P. (2017). "Neural regulation of endocrine and
    autonomic stress responses". Nature Reviews Neuroscience. 10 (6): pp.
    397–409. doi:10.1038/nrn2647. ISSN 1471-003X. PMC 4240627 Freely
    accessible. PMID 19469025.

Warner, C. H.; Bobo, W.; Warner, C.; Reid, S.; & Rachal, J. (2006).
    "Antidepressant discontinuation syndrome". American Family Physician.
    74 (3): pp. 449–56. PMID 16913164.

Wu, H.-C. (2005). "Continuum mechanics and plasticity". Boca Raton:
    Chapman & Hall/CRC Press. pp. 45-132. ISBN 978-1-58488-363-0.

INDEX:

The Mental Illness Handbook

9 781979 284783